T0031940

INVESTIGATING THE ABOMINABLE SNOWMAN
AND OTHER LEGENDARY BEASTS

JEANNE NAGLE

Britannica
Educational Publishing

IN ASSOCIATION WITH

ROSEN
EDUCATIONAL SERVICES

Published in 2015 by Britannica Educational Publishing (a trademark of Encyclopædia Britannica, Inc.) in association with The Rosen Publishing Group, Inc.
29 East 21st Street, New York, NY 10010

Distributed exclusively by Rosen Publishing.
To see additional Britannica Educational Publishing titles, go to rosenpublishing.com.

First Edition

Britannica Educational Publishing
J. E. Luebering: Director, Core Reference Group
Anthony L. Green: Editor, Compton's by Britannica

Rosen Publishing
Hope Lourie Killcoyne: Executive Editor
Nelson Sá: Art Director
Nicole Russo: Designer
Cindy Reiman: Photography Manager

Library of Congress Cataloging-in-Publication Data

Nagle, Jeanne.
Investigating the abominable snowman and other legendary beasts/Jeanne Nagle.—First Edition.
    pages cm.—(Understanding the paranormal)
Includes bibliographical references and index.
ISBN 978-1-62275-853-1 (library bound) — ISBN 978-1-62275-854-8 (pbk.) —
ISBN 978-1-62275-855-5 (6-pack)
1. Yeti—Juvenile literature. 2. Animals, Mythical—Juvenile literature. I. Title.
QL89.2.Y4N34 2014
001.944—dc23

                                                                    2014023131

Manufactured in the United States of America

CONTENTS

INTRODUCTION

A people known as the Sherpas traditionally have treated the Himalayas, the mountains where they live, as sacred. They have built Buddhist monasteries at the mountains' base, placing prayer flags on the slopes, and establishing sanctuaries, or safe spaces, for the wildlife of the valleys. For these reasons, the Sherpas have shown the mountains great respect, and for many years they would not climb them.

Mixed with their respect was a good amount of wonder and fear. For one thing, the Sherpas did not want to disturb or anger the gods and demons that were believed to live up in the high peaks. Also keeping them away was a mysterious creature that supposedly roamed the mountains' lower slopes: the yeti, or the so-called Abominable Snowman.

A legendary creature, the Abominable Snowman is said to live in the Himalayas above the snow line. Although several attempts have been made to sight it, the creature has so far proved elusive, or hard to find. A lack of credible evidence has not kept stories about the yeti from being shared around the world. Some people insist that the creature—as well as other legendary beasts around the world—exists, while other people work to disprove, or debunk, the myths. Regardless, the search for the truth about the Abominable Snowman and other yeti-like creatures continues.

Prayer flags strung near a Buddhist shrine in Ladakh, in the Indian Himalayas. There have been reported yeti sightings in the region.

CHAPTER ONE

MAN-BEAST OF THE FROZEN HEIGHTS

S tories about unusual animals were commonplace in earlier times. Such animals are called legendary because they exist only in these stories, or legends. The stories were often based on travelers' reports of animals that were unfamiliar to them. Some famous legendary animals include the dragon, various sea serpents, the unicorn, and the phoenix.

Other legendary creatures resemble humans yet are not quite human. Even today some people speak of having seen these half-human, half-animal creatures, including the yeti, better known as the Abominable Snowman.

APPEARANCE

The word *abominable* means hateful or strongly unpleasant. That term is applied to the yeti mainly because it is said to look very fierce and scary. The creature is covered from head to toe in long, messy fur. Some people think that the creature is called a snowman because its fur is white. However, that assumption seems to be false. People who claim to have seen it say that the fur is actually a reddish brown color. So the yeti is called a snowman not because of its color but rather because of the weather conditions where it is believed to live.

Various stories have given different measurements for how big and tall the Abominable Snowman

Drawing of a yeti. With a human chest and body hair all over, this image shows why yetis are called man-beasts.

is. Everyone seems to agree, however, that the creature is at least six feet (about two meters) tall. Some stories claim that it is two to four feet (about a half meter to a little over a meter) taller than that.

People who say they have seen the Abominable Snowman are able to guess at its height because, apparently, the creature walks on two legs, like a human. Yet some accounts discuss how sometimes it gets down on all fours, meaning it uses its arms as legs, when running or moving quickly. Still other stories note that the creature places the knuckles of its hands on the ground, so that it moves sort of like an ape or gorilla.

COUSIN OF THE WOODS

This is the well-known freeze-frame of the famous Patterson-Gimlin film from 1967, which supposedly captured a Bigfoot in midstride in the hills next to Bluff Creek, in the wilderness near Orleans, in Northern California.

Bigfoot, or Sasquatch, is supposed to be a lot like a yeti. The creature is thought by some to live in the northwestern United States and western Canada. Bigfoot has been described as being anywhere from 6 to 15 feet (2 to 4.5 meters) tall, standing up and walking on two feet. Some people say it lets out a cry, while others say it doesn't make a sound. Bigfoot is supposed to smell bad as well. Despite many claims of sightings—of mysterious footprints or of the beast itself—most scientists do not believe that Bigfoot exists.

LOCATION

The Abominable Snowman is said to roam the Himalayan slopes of Kanchenjunga, the world's third-highest mountain. The mountain is in the Indian state of Sikkim, located in the northeastern part of the country, along the border with Nepal. Some two-thirds of the state consists of mountains that are snow-covered year-round.

The area has long been considered sacred, which means holy. Buddhist monasteries have been built at the

The snowy peak of Mt. Kanchenjunga (right), the alleged Himalayan home of the Abominable Snowman.

base of the mountains, and the Sherpas place prayer flags on the slopes. Just below the timberline, or the place on a mountain slope where tree growth stops, is where the Abominable Snowman is said to live. Forests near the timberline offer a place for the yeti to hide when it is not out on the slopes looking for food.

THE SHERPAS

The Sherpas are a group of some 50,000 mountain-dwelling people, most of whom live in the Asian country of Nepal; Sikkim state, India; and Tibet, a region of China. The term *Sherpas* also refers to people of this region (not necessarily ethnic Sherpas) who have excellent mountain-climbing and hiking skills. Until the twentieth century, Sherpas had not attempted to climb the Himalayas, which they viewed as the home of the gods. Fear of the Abominable Snowman, which many Sherpas have reported seeing, had also kept them off the slopes, despite their mountain-climbing skills. (In Sikkim the Abominable Snowman is called Nee-gued; in various regions of Asia the name Almas is used.)

A Sherpa carries a pack as he prepares to take part in an expedition up Mt. Everest, in Nepal.

YETI FOOD

The Abominable Snowman has been reported to be an omnivore, which means it eats just about anything, animals and plants. However, emphasis is placed on the yeti as a meat eater.

In the valleys of Mount Kanchenjunga live animals such as musk deer, pheasants, and Himalayan partridge. Herders also take their sheep and goats up the mountain to graze, or eat grass. While the yeti has not been known to hunt birds, there are many stories of deer, yaks, and livestock being attacked and eaten by the creature.

Yaks grazing in the foothills of Mount Kanchenjunga. The animals are supposed to be a favorite item on a yeti's menu.

Human beings do not appear to be on the yeti's menu. Stories exist about the Abominable Snowman scaring or attacking humans, but no one has ever claimed that a person was eaten by the monster.

ONE OR MANY?

Legends speak of one giant creature called the Abominable Snowman. However, the Sherpas say there are many yetis living in the Himalayan woods, and each is one of two main types of yeti.

The larger of the two types, known as *dzu-ti*, is reported to be about ten feet (three meters) tall. The *dzu-ti*

is supposed to be aggressive, or willing to attack, and is therefore considered more dangerous. The other type, called *meh-ti* by the Sherpas, is smaller and calmer. Supposedly the meh-ti is a bit shy and runs away if it comes across a human.

If one believes in the Abominable Snowman, common sense would seem to prove that there is more than

In this drawing of a yeti sighting, the creature appears to be running away from the climbers, meaning it would most likely be a meh-ti.

one yeti. Stories about the creature have been around since ancient times. To be around that long, younger yetis would have to have been born as the older ones died. (This would also mean that there are female yetis, even though the creatures are called "snowmen.") The

YE-RÉN: THE WILD MAN OF EAST ASIA

In the Chinese language Mandarin, Ye-Rén means "wild man." Actually, wild men would seem more apt, as there appear to be two types of these creatures that some claim to exist—one that walks on two feet and one that walks on four. Some people claim to have sighted a red-haired, primate-like creature which they described as smiling and chatty. Scientific analysis of alleged Ye-Rén hairs report that they "derive from a higher primate not yet known to zoology."

A stone marker near the forested area of China, in Hubei province, where Ye-Rén are said to live.

only other explanation would be that the Abominable Snowman is immortal, which means it lives forever. Claiming that it is immortal would certainly point to the yeti being a legendary creature, instead of real.

CHAPTER TWO

EXPEDITION: ABOMINABLE!

The legend of the Abominable Snowman has been around a long time, especially in Eastern cultures. A bear-like creature known as a *fei-fei* is mentioned in ancient Chinese writings, and myths about a similar creature have been told in Nepal and India for centuries. Sightings and stories started to be told by Westerners in the 1800s.

EARLY WESTERN STORIES AND SIGHTINGS

The first mention of the Abominable Snowman by someone from the West happened in 1832. A British explorer named Brian Houghton Hodgson was studying the people and animals of Nepal, including those in the mountains. He wrote about the time people who

Brian Houghton Hodgson, the first Westerner to call attention to the possible existence of yetis.

were working for him were chased by something large and hairy. Hodgson himself did not see the creature. He thought it might be an orangutan, which is a type of large ape.

Almost sixty years later, another British explorer reported seeing strange tracks in the snow of the Himalayas. L. A. Waddell, who was a soldier and teacher as well as an explorer, had heard stories about the yeti from people living in the area. Even after talking to people who had supposedly seen the creature, Waddell didn't believe it existed. When he and his workers found unusual footprints in the snow, the workers said they were yeti prints. Waddell, however, believed the tracks were made by a "snowbear," which he assumed to be a large bear that lives in the snowy mountains.

THE FLORIDA SKUNK APE

Bigfoot, also known as Sasquatch, has been described as residing in the northwestern United States and western Canada. So what happens if sightings of a somewhat similar being occur in Florida? For one thing, it gets its own name: skunk ape. (Why skunk? Apparently, its stench is epic.) Floridians aplenty report sightings; one website devoted to the alleged Everglades dweller receives several sightings a week, some from beyond the Everglades. But while the skunk ape has many who believe in its existence, the people who work for the United States National Park Service are not among them.

Picture of what some claim is a skunk ape, photographed near Sarasota, Florida, in 2000. Sarasota is north of the Everglades, where most skunk apes are supposed to hide in the swamps.

THE EVEREST CONNECTION

The highest point on Earth, Mount Everest is one of the Himalayas of southern Asia. Mount Everest has long been a challenge to mountaineers. Early attempts to reach the summit began in the 1920s. During the first British expedition up Everest in 1921, hikers found tracks in the snow that they could not explain. The English climbers guessed that at that height—20,000 (6,000 meters) feet up the mountain—the tracks were made by a large grey wolf. The tracks were so large, they thought, because a wolf might have walked with its back paws in the same prints that its front paws made. Sherpas on the trip claimed the footprints were made by a yeti.

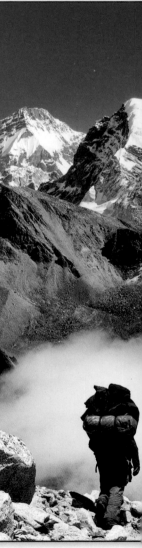

The leader of the 1921 trip, a man named C. K. Howard-Bury, wrote a book about the experience. In this book, Howard-Bury first used the words "abominable snowman" to describe the yeti. Experts believe he misunderstood the Nepalese name for the creature, which actually meant something like "man-bear snow creature." The Nepalese never called it "abominable" or anything like that. Howard-Bury also wrote that he thought the story of the creature was a made-up "fairy tale," meant to scare little children into being good.

In 1951 another group tried climbing to the top of Mount Everest. This team, led by British explorer Eric Shipton, did not make it to the peak, but they became

A mountain climber looking at the towering Mt. Everest. Strange tracks on Everest's slopes, found starting in 1921, had some people wondering if a yeti was in the area.

famous for another reason. Shipton and the other climbers came upon large tracks in the snow. This time, however, instead of just writing about the discovery, they took pictures of the prints. The story and the pictures made their way into newspapers around the world. People everywhere became very interested in the Abominable Snowman.

One of the snowprints found on Everest by an expedition led by Eric Shipton in 1951. The pickaxe is placed below to show the track's size.

THE HUNT IS ON

In 1954—a year after a group of climbers finally reached the top of Mount Everest—the London newspaper the *Daily Mail* paid for an expedition that became a yeti hunt. Hundreds of people, including scientists and professional climbers, took part in the three-month expedition. In addition to climbing Everest, their goal was to find proof that yetis existed.

The climbers found more footprints but not much else to help prove the Abominable Snowman existed. However, articles and pictures of the expedition that appeared in the *Daily Mail* made other people and organizations want to join the search. One of those people was a wealthy oilman from Texas named Tom Slick, who paid for at least two expeditions to find a yeti.

The government of Nepal almost put a stop to Slick's first expedition, in 1957, before it even started. Nepalese officials would not let the search happen unless they could be sure that the team had official, reliable backing.

Graphic image of explorer Tom Slick, showing a yeti in the background. Slick spent years trying to prove whether or not yetis were real.

YETIS FOR SALE

The people of Nepal made the most of how popular the Abominable Snowman had become. Nepalese vacation ads of the late 1950s listed yetis as well as Mount Everest as things that tourists should see. At first the country's government made it illegal to hunt or shoot yetis. But then officials started selling hunting permits for thousands of dollars. Experts think that the government did not believe anyone would ever shoot or kill a yeti. Therefore, they weren't at risk for losing one of the country's best tourist attractions.

Slick got the San Antonio (Texas) Zoo to support the expedition.

Instead of hunting and shooting yetis, Slick and his team hoped to catch one of the creatures alive. They even had a special trap built. Maybe they thought that the San Antonio Zoo could put the yeti on display. We'll never know because, obviously, the team never caught the legendary creature.

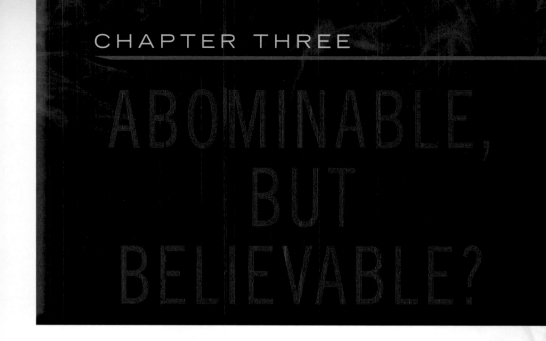

CHAPTER THREE

ABOMINABLE, BUT BELIEVABLE?

Expeditions supported by Tom Slick and the *Daily Mail* did not find the Abominable Snowman. However, both groups did come across what they believed was evidence that yetis existed. Team members from both expeditions visited Buddhist monasteries high in the Himalayas and saw what monks claimed were yeti hair, skin, and body parts. (The monks thought such items were sacred because they were

A fur sample believed by some to come from a yeti rests in a locked box in a place of honor in a Himalayan Buddhist monastery.

DO NOT MESS WITH MESSNER

Adventurer Reinhold Messner was famous for, among other things, encountering a yeti while traveling through the Himalayas.

The Italian mountaineer Reinhold Messner was famous for many daring feats, including climbing Everest by himself without using bottled oxygen. One night in 1986, Messner crossed paths with a large creature in a Himalayan valley. The creature ran away but left large footprints behind. Messner spent the next ten years, and several more trips up into the mountains, trying to figure out if he had seen the Abominable Snowman. His research led to the conclusion that yetis do not exist but instead are actually bears that live in the mountains.

found on the mountains, which were considered holy ground.) In both these cases, scientific testing proved that the sacred relics, or holy objects, kept by the monks actually came from other animals.

Testing has advanced quite a bit since the 1950s. Today, scientists have the ability to conduct very accurate DNA tests on items of unknown origin.

EDMUND HILLARY ON THE TRAIL

At 11:30 AM on May 29, 1953, New Zealand mountaineer Edmund Hillary and the Tibetan porter Tenzing Norgay reached the 29,035-foot (8,850 m) summit of Mount Everest. They were the first people to make it to the top of the world's highest mountain.

In 1960, Hillary took on a new challenge in the Himalayas. While on an expedition to study the effects of cold and high altitude on mountain climbers, he also did a little investigating into the legend of the Abominable Snowman.

Hillary and his team found unusually large tracks in the snow, as other climbers had done before. That said, the group did not just accept that these were yeti footprints. They realized that animal tracks and human footprints get larger as the snow in which they are made starts to melt in the sun. The expedition members decided that the prints they had found were actually the partly melted

(Left to right) Sir Edmund Hillary and Tenzing Norgay. Hillary helped debunk yeti rumors by sharing a logical reason behind unusual prints his climbers found on Mt. Everest.

tracks of an animal, maybe a snow leopard or a bear.

Members of the expedition also examined fur and two scalps that were supposed to come from yetis. After testing, the fur was proven to be that of a bear, and the scalps were fakes made from the skin and fur of a serow, a mammal that looks like a fuzzy goat.

LENDING A HAND TO RESEARCH

In 2011, scientists solved a sixty-year-old mystery involving yetis, a Buddhist monastery, and a single, mummified finger. The finger came from a supposed yeti hand from a monastery in

Skin, fur, and bones from the Pangboche monastery in Nepal were later proven to come from a bear (scalp) and human (hand), not a yeti.

Pangboche, Nepal, kept by monks who believed it was a sacred relic. The hand was discovered in 1959 by a man named Peter Byrne, who was working with none other than the millionaire adventurer Tom Slick.

Finding the hand was pretty easy. After all, many monasteries in the Himalayas have such items. Proving whether or not it belonged to a yeti was a little more difficult. The monks did not want to let Byrne and Slick take the hand back to England. Byrne convinced the monks to part with one finger, which eventually ended up at the Royal College of Surgeons in London.

A FINGER POINTS THE WAY

There are different versions of how "the Pangboche finger" found its way to a museum in London. The most popular story is that Peter Byrne swapped a human finger from a different museum for the supposed yeti one, also offering the monks money. At the time it was illegal to take items such as the finger out of Nepal. The rumor is that Byrne convinced American actor Jimmy Stewart, who was vacationing nearby in India, to smuggle the finger out of the country inside his luggage.

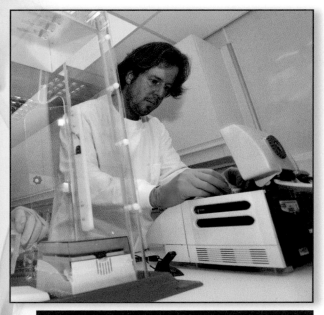

A scientist at work at the Royal Zoological Society of Scotland.

Museum workers who were cataloging items, meaning checking a list of the museum's possessions, discovered the finger and decided to do some testing on it. Testing by a genetics expert at the Royal Zoological Society of Scotland showed that it had human DNA. In other words, the finger and the hand it had come from belonged to a human being, not the legendary Snowman.

THE CASE OF THE RUSSIAN YETI

In 2011 a team of scientists from the United States was invited to Russia to examine evidence and help confirm that a yeti existed in the region of Siberia. The trip was billed as a "yeti conference." The scientists were taken to a cave near a poor mining town, where their hosts showed them a supposed "nest," or bed, said to belong to a yeti. Footprints around the entrance to the cave and a hair sample were also offered as evidence of the creature's existence.

One of the American scientists, anthropologist and college professor Jeff Meldrum, has since confirmed that he felt the Russian evidence was completely made up and part of a hoax. The Russian citizens involved were not scientists themselves, and they wanted actual scientists to sign papers stating that the yeti was real. Meldrum and others believe the Russians were merely trying to create publicity and get tourists to spend money at the supposed yeti site.

THE DNA OF ANCIENT BEARS

Advances in DNA research continue. Today, scientists have the ability to conduct very accurate DNA tests on items of unknown origin. That is exactly what British geneticist Bryan Sykes did in 2013 regarding animal pelts that were said to come from a yeti.

Sykes, who worked at Oxford University in England, was part of a team—along with members from the Lausanne Museum of Zoology in Switzerland—that was created to provide genetic testing to samples supposedly derived from yetis. Using samples from an Indian region of the Himalayas and from Bhutan, the research team compared the DNA from chunks of hair to samples in

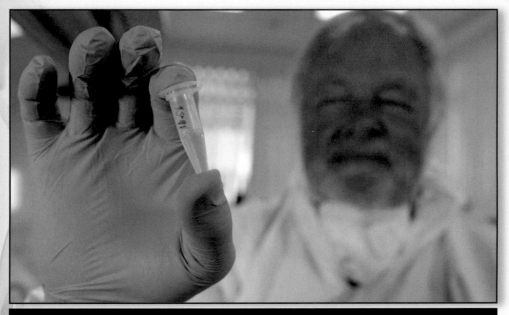

Geneticist Bryan Sykes, showing a sample of hair supposedly from a yeti, in 2013. Sykes's testing proved that the hair actually came from a member of the bear family.

an international database. Scientists discovered a perfect match. To what? A type of polar bear that lived in Norway up to 120,000 years ago.

Obviously the fur did not come directly from a long-ago animal; one sample was forty years old and the other was only ten years old. Scientific evidence led Sykes and other scientists on the research team to conclude that the fur came from a cross between a descendant of an ancient polar bear and a Himalayan brown bear. Many people thought yetis could have actually been bears. The DNA testing seems to prove them right.

CHAPTER FOUR

FAMED IN STORY AND SONG

T here is a well-known story about a teenager in Nepal seeing what could have been the Abominable Snowman in 1974. Lhakpa Domani was with her family's herd of yaks near Mount Everest when she heard a strange noise. When she turned around she came face-to-face with what she said was a yeti. The creature grabbed her and threw her into a stream, then killed some of her yaks before stomping away.

This story has become famous because many newspapers and television shows about

Actress Felicity Huffman, posing with the title character from the animated video Choose Your Own Adventure: The Abominable Snowman. *Huffman provided a voice for the video, released in 2006.*

mysterious creatures have featured it since the 1970s. It has become part of the cryptozoology culture. The Abominable Snowman has become part of the world's popular culture through Lhakpa's story and in many other ways.

TELEVISED YETIS

About the time that yeti-seeking expeditions in the Himalayas became popular, the Abominable Snowman made its first appearance on television. A televised play called "The Creature" was shown as part of the program *BBC Sunday-Night Theatre* on January 30, 1955, in England. The plot involves two scientists searching the Himalayas for a yeti. One scientist wants to find the creature to prove that it is related to humans. The other wants to trap a yeti and make people pay to see it on display. Eventually all the humans except the good scientist are killed by a group of angry yetis using strange powers of their minds, not their strength.

The Abominable Snowman also showed up on the animated holiday movie-for-television *Rudolf the Red-Nosed Reindeer* (1964). The scary creature is eventually tamed by a character who calls him a "Bumble." Many young children in the United States first learned about the Abominable Snowman by watching this show.

These two examples, as well as a handful more, show the Abominable Snowman for fun and entertainment. However, yetis have been the subject of more serious television investigations as well. In 1997, the History Channel aired an episode of their *In Search of History* series that

Action figures from the animated Christmas special Rudolf the Red-Nosed Reindeer. *The Abominable Snowman* (far left) *was a villain in the special.*

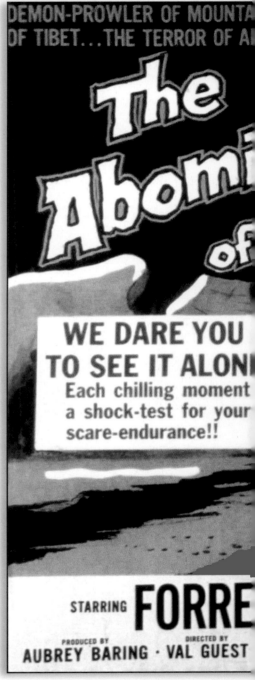

looked into whether or not yetis existed. In 2011, National Geographic released a DVD titled *Hunt for the Abominable Snowman*.

BIG-SCREEN APPEARANCES

In the 1950s, just as yetis were becoming extremely popular, three movies about the Abominable Snowman hit theaters. *The Snow Creature* (1954) had botanists (scientists who study plants) finding a yeti family in the Himalayas and bringing the father back to Los Angeles. The 1956 film *Man-Beast* focused not only on yetis living in the mountains but a scientist who turns out to be half-yeti himself. *The Abominable Snowman of the Himalayas* (1957) was a feature-film version of the BBC television play "The Creature." In 2013, a company called Hammer Films announced that it was going to remake this movie, making it a bit more modern.

A poster promoting the movie Abominable Snowman of the Himalayas, *which thrilled moviegoers in 1957.*

FUN AND GAMES

In Nepal and other locations near the Himalayan mountains, the legend of the yeti has been used to help young children behave: "Be good or the yeti will come and carry you away." It is interesting, then, that children's toys are another way in which yetis have become part of popular culture, particularly in North America.

In 1963 Louis Marx and Company included the Abominable Snowman in its Gallery of Monsters line of action figures. The mini hairy beast, which operated with batteries and a remote control, walked, raised its arms, and, according to the box, let out a cry described as a "shriek." In the 1970s, Mego Corporation sold an Abominable Snowman action figure as part of its Famous Monsters of Legend series. Tomland, which was part of the Marx toy company, issued a copycat figure shortly after the Mego version came out. The makers of G.I. Joe created action-figure sets that featured yetis in 1973 and 2002.

Beyond action figures, the Abominable Snowman has been part of several video games, including *World of Warcraft* and *Zelda: Twilight Princess*. The creature even has his own themed video games, including *Urban Yeti* and the online flash game *YetiSports*. Also, artist and designer Tim Biskup created a yeti character that appeared on everything from glasses and key chains to T-shirts, wallets, and slippers.

Jedi wannabes attack a yeti-like Wampa ice creature outside a Florida toy store during a Star Wars–themed event in 2010.

ABOMINABLE BY THE BOOK

Mount Everest explorers wrote about the legendary Abominable Snowman in brief while telling their stories about mountain climbing. Taking their cue from

BOOGIE DOWN, BUMBLE

A few songs have been written about yetis and the Abominable Snowman. Most are novelty songs, which means they are supposed to be funny. Novelty yeti songs include "Abominable Snowman in the Market" (1977) and "The Yeti Song" (1982). The children's program *The Backyardigans* also had a minor hit with its "Yeti Stomp" (2004).

these real-life adventures, the creator of the popular twentieth-century cartoon character Tintin created a storyline where the hero goes to Tibet and finds a yeti. The book *Tintin in Tibet* was published in 1960.

Since then, many books about the Abominable Snowman and yetis in general have appeared in print. These range from serious investigations into whether or not yetis exist to fun reading. Books about yetis have been written for all age groups, even preschoolers (*Betty and the Yeti*; 2010).

A QUESTION OF PROOF

Movies, television shows, and books are just stories, not proof. For instance, some people have found large

Many a reader has enjoyed the books of Belgian cartoonist Hergé, which detail the adventures of Tintin, including the character's journey to Tibet and his encounter with a yeti.

tracks in the mountains, which they believed were made by the Abominable Snowman. A number of people have said that they have caught sight of the creatures. Some witnesses claim to have proof in the form of photos or videos. However, most people think such images are either unclear or fake.

When trying to be scientific about yetis, some people have argued that these mysterious creatures could be rare primates, or an ancient type of ape. Others have said they could be the living descendants of

Bob Gimlin (left) and Roger Patterson, posing in 1967 with casts they claim to have made of Bigfoot tracks. The two said they had seen and filmed the legendary creature.

prehistoric humans, such as Neanderthals. But most scientists think those explanations are unlikely. And, as scientific analyses of various samples have proven, the legend of the Abominable Snowman as well as other legendary beasts is just that: legend. The fact is that so far no undeniable, scientific proof for the existence of the Abominable Snowman—or any other legendary beast—exists. Until that time—if it ever comes—it is very safe to conclude that these creatures are indeed merely myth and legend.

GLOSSARY

ABOMINABLE Very bad or unpleasant.

ANTHROPOLOGIST One who studies the origins, societies, and cultures of the human race.

CRYPTOZOOLOGY The study of and search for legendary animals.

DEBUNK To prove that a belief is false.

EXPEDITION A journey especially by a group of people for a specific purpose.

IMMORTAL Someone or something that will live forever.

LEGENDARY Used to describe a story from a long time ago that cannot be proven true.

MONASTERY A place where monks work and live together.

MOUNTAINEER A person who climbs mountains.

MUMMIFIED Something that has become very dry and wrinkled with age.

PHOENIX A legendary bird that is said to have burned in a fire but rose alive from the ashes.

PRIMATE Any member of the group of animals that includes human beings, apes, and monkeys.

PUBLICITY Something that attracts the attention of many people.

ROAM To go to different places without any sort of plan.

SHERPA A member of a group of people who live in the Himalayas; also describes someone who leads mountain climbers up Himalayan peaks.

SMUGGLE To move something secretly and often illegally from one country to another.

TAME To make something less wild and more accustomed and comfortable in the presence of people.

ZOOLOGY A branch of science that involves the study of real animals.

FOR FURTHER READING

BOOKS

Anderson, Jennifer Joline. *Bigfoot and Yeti* (Creatures of Legend). Minneapolis, MN: Core Library (ABDO), 2014.

Colson, Mary. *Bigfoot and the Yeti*. Los Angeles, CA: Ignite Publishing, 2013.

Emmer, Rick. *Bigfoot: Fact or Fiction?* New York, NY: Chelsea House Publishers, 2010.

Hand, Carol. *The Existence of Sasquatch and Yeti*. Minneapolis, MN: Essential Library (ABDO), 2012.

Rajczak, Kristen. *Climbing Mount Everest*. New York, NY: Gareth Stevens, 2014.

Regan, Lisa, and Chris McNab. *Urban Myths and Legendary Creatures*. New York, NY: Gareth Stevens, 2011.

Roberts, Steven. *The Yeti*. New York, NY: PowerKids Press, 2012.

WEBSITES

Because of the changing nature of Internet links, Rosen Publishing has developed an online list of websites related to the subject of this book. This site is updated regularly. Please use this link to access the list:

http://www.rosenlinks.com/UTP/Abom

INDEX